PASSIFLORA

Cider Press Review

PO Box 33384, San Diego, CA 92163   www.ciderpressreview.com

Dear *CPR* Book Award Contest Entrant:

Thank you for your participation in the 2019 *Cider Press Review* Book Award. Enclosed, please find your copy of the 2019 winning book, *Passiflora*, by Kathy Davis.

The Editors' Prize Book Award opens to submission on April 1, 2021. All entrants will receive a copy of the winning book. Visit ciderpressreview.com/bookaward for more details.

Sincerely,

Caron Andregg
Publisher

Beth McDermott
Editor-in-Chief

passiflora

poems

Kathy Davis

Cider Press Review
San Diego

Cider Press Review
PO BOX 33384
San Diego, CA, 92163 USA
ciderpressreview.com

First edition
10 9 8 7 6 5 4 3 2 1 0

ISBN: 9781930781580
Library of Congress Control Number: 2021953054
Cover photo courtesy Rawpixel
Author photograph by Grace Kellogg
Additional Images: "Passion Flower (1825) by Jean Bernard (1775-
1883)." Original from The Rijksmuseum. Digitally enhanced/
modified by rawpixel and Caron Andregg; "Antique plant drawn by
Pierre-Joseph Redouté(1759-1840)." Digitally enhanced/modified
by rawpixel and Caron Andregg
Book design by Caron Andregg

Winner of the 2019 Cider Press Review Book Award:
ciderpressreview.com/bookaward.

Printed in the United States of America
at Bookmobile in Minneapolis, MN USA.

For my parents, Hoke & Sara
And for Bob, Bryson & Mick

Contents

Red passion flower (Passiflora racemosa)

How to Grow Wild

Vision failing, she feels the leaves,
looking for butterfly weed, a seedling
from her greenhouse for me to take
in my efforts to flower a field.
Cup plant, sweet goldenrod.
Stratify the seeds six weeks,
then scratch them in—instructions
on the packets she presses
in my hands, stressing
the importance of natives.

On this street of manicured lawns,
her home, the yard not mown,
could be mistaken for abandoned.
Fleabane, milkweed. But no monarchs
this summer so far—a hint
of loss that worries her. *Invasive,*
she says about the swamp
sunflower. *You may curse me*
for giving it to you. My mother's
death still fresh, her daughter
decades buried, she is showing me

how to grow wild, which takes
planning: *Don't let it go*
natural. You'll have a mess
of wire grass with very little bloom.
No tilling or compost—
the seeds, tissue thin, prefer hard,
poor soil. Little blue stem

should be mixed in. Rudbeckia,
too bright and dominant,
will need to be thinned. And once
a year, to discourage saplings,
burn the whole lot down to the ground.

Starlings

A black hand across the landscape, then thousands
rummaging the corn's winter wreckage.

They rise and clap, swarm, recede. Black is one
of only three proper colors—brown,

and white, the others—for a lady's gloves, Mother
claimed. The hands touching lightly now as if

out of concern. Her favorite this black
motion, the trees swept bare except for a surge

of birds. The suicide in the blue room
kept from us for years, the box in the attic

nailed shut. We knew enough, she thought, her children.
How to fold napkins in thirds, not halves, spoon

soup away from us. Her own mother careful
to cut faces from the photographs. Sweeping

up, I find ten centimes, a jack,
the flock now roosting overhead. She believed

in travel. The cacophony of song
a hellish choir, each bird's tune slightly off

from the rest. It's been years since I've been back,
the lies elaborate and smart, the silence

beyond the rush of wings above—a slack
gate swinging on its hinges. Let it slap

away. I know how to set a proper
table, knives always on the right, blades always

facing in. Death rejoices to teach the living
answers I no longer care to know.

The field's a blank and sure to fill again.

For My Son's Birth Mother

i. Bird

— installation by Lael Corbin

The clues are few, the quiet
eerie, the scientist missing
from this lab. Whatever work
was being done here

is unfinished—ribs of a fuselage
suspended from the ceiling, petri dishes
abloom, a scattering of sketches—
abandoned on the threshold

of discovery. Will he return?
You knew it was a boy
the nurses whisked away,

then nothing more.

ii. watching, waiting, commiserating

—sculptured installation by Ruben Ochoa

They seem to defy gravity,
these creatures, pallets that tower
dangerously high on a forest
of spider legs. The twists and turns

of each fragile limb suggesting
a tender dance, an enchanted
wood. But daylight filters through
and parses the real

from the imagined. These "legs" are built
of rebar, firm, cemented to the floor.
For B., you are the whimsical ballet,

and I, the common steel.

iii. Floating Female

—video in the round by Lærke Lauta

Upside down in a tree, hanging
like fruit or bats, three white-feathered
girls asleep. The leaves, the girls' dark curls
and fluff of birdskins slightly ruffled

by a breeze. To the left, one of their kind
floats face down in the pond, as if
blown there by a storm. Turn,
and there's a gathering of mourners. Turn

again, an old woman in red frowns
out over the water. They are beautiful,
the girls, ripe for the plucking.

iv. Rise and Fall

— video installation by Fiona Tan

Two screens braid time—before, after,
after, before—and a young woman
and old, who are perhaps the same person,
going through the motions

of an ordinary day. At times they stare off,
deep in thought, as if each is trying to imagine
the other. The camera
breaks away—a river churns

until it tumbles into a void—

                     I can hear the roar.
B. on his own now, a man. The two women
wander the same garden

in different seasons, searching for a boy.

Weeding

In the back garden, habaneros   broken
    shade over what's forgotten
        from breakfast   shells, grounds

on the rot of old clippings
    volunteer corn   holding an isolated thought
        against the breeze   *Where*

is that child?   I was trying to remember
    the French for strawberry   the precise hour
        of blue on the china

Absurd the haphazard filings
    a mind rifles   the drunk selling nosegays
        old directions to Orient Beach

Wire grass, insidious
    spreads the bed   evening
        primrose in the spirea   *He should have*

called by now   pigweed sprouting   here
    there   a deep breath   take it   clover
        tiny shoots beneath the juniper

The trick is painting
    my neighbor likes to explain   herbicide
        a brush application

dribbles down the stalk   to the root
    a brown country   the stiff-handed dead
        weeds   waving from her yard   *I shouldn't*

have   *let him go*   parting narrow and arching
    blades of liriope   I pluck an invasion of wild
        onions   pungent and sweet

My spade hacks   a tangle of roots   the nerve ends
    tremble   tiny clods of dirt   hanging on
        The word *fraise*   drifts up

Late Summer

I go through his things, look for stories,
poems no one's seen in print before. The boxes
piled high in a nook upstairs, paintings stacked
and leaning against the wall. *I'm writing*
like a motherfucker, and I don't know why,
he wrote just months before
he died, suddenly. Dust, dust and stars,
images he was working and re-working, snow
and fire. What does the body know? At twenty,
I circled stanchions in a museum, convinced
the woman inside was real. Stiff
in a ladderback chair, gray hair curled
trigger tight, she stared down at her hands folded
in her lap. I tried to catch her breathing, make
her laugh. Blew on her neck, snapped fingers
under her nose, pulled my face into gargoyle grins,
until one eye toward the guard, I stretched out
a hand, hovered a second over her arm,
then quick, tag, you're it. She was hard, cold
statue. Outside, the wind whipped against
the building, shaking the plate glass. And here:
a random thought on a bar napkin, a nasty note
from an ex-wife, so many sheets of paper,
yellow pads, a rush of cursive and his name,
first and last, in the top right corner of each page.

Wake

The snow globe shaken so hard
trees and people float loose above
the tiny alpine village. An unappealing
afterlife, heaven in a knickknack,
although no one still stuck
seems to notice, each holding
the same pose they had before.

Undone

Borage leaves for courage, heart,
but I harvest just the blossoms, layer them

in plastic clamshells. Squint, they're blue
sky in a box. The black anthers,

a murder of crows. Bones sometimes
surface in the compost. A sheep's skull

over the greenhouse door. The farmer
down the road never mucked his stalls,

left ewes, lambs to rot where they fell. *Garden,*
I thought when he died. Took a shovel

to the rich dark mix, hauled it and his
abandoned collie home. The flower

tastes like cucumber. Watery, bland. Pleasure
mostly in the color. Each day, nosing the path

back to the old man's, the collie sits at the end
of her undone chain. The way—out of longing,

duty, habit—I've worried my own dead.
Time and worms and heat have worked

the stench from the manure. My hands
gentle, the dog cowers, still anticipating blows.

No Rain for a Spell

I know he's coming, the man with the tractor,
so many fields around me harvested
already. Flower heads close to bursting on the timothy
out back, and here and there the reach of purple
clover, dandelion. Sometimes he cuts

the crop at night, headlights rude
through the bedroom window. The blade and rake
laying down row after row while I attempt
to sleep. Field mice and nesting birds in flight,
and you by my side, dreaming

undisturbed. He is taking, you would say,
what's his. The hay left for days to dry
before it's baled and hauled away. Horses
bending in their stalls to feed. I know a woman
who gathers summer weeds, weaves them

into bundles with buttons, needle, thread. Winter,
when the muse lurks in pod and root,
she presses pigment from the remnants,
brushes the meadow onto sheets of homemade
English ivy paper. Once in a foreign city,

you snuck us past an armored tank to reach
the restaurant in the alley just beyond. I can't
remember what we ate, only the warm *bienvenue*
of the chef's embrace, the lusty zest
with which he delivered food, plates laddered

up his arms, the sound of silver scraping dish
as we took in what he had to give.

Sunday

Joan leans over
the fence, says she had a mastectomy
last Tuesday. And I think: A meal,

I should have known
and taken her one. Chicken tetrazzini,
tossed salad. She winces when I touch

her arm. A wasp,
for a moment, gives us both something
to wave at. Any degree of mobility

increases survival. *What can I do?*
I ask, knowing the answer
will be *Nothing.* Tomatoes, onions, squash

to be chopped.
On my kitchen table, the knife
I use to cut everything in little squares. A breeze,

from somewhere the scent of honeysuckle.
Let me know if you need
anything, I say. Joan's face blank.

The zinnias shouting red. She nods, weaves
gingerly back inside. Her screen door
misses the latch, hangs open like a dare.

Ruins, Trophies, Palms

Go back inside, my neighbor calls,
there's a wolf at the end of your drive.
She hits the buttons
on her alarm system.
A man's voice: *windows and doors*
secure. I stay where I am,
listening. He's too big
for my small hands—
Schumann, his chords.
But someone is playing—
a lilt, a leap, a land.
The scream of a small rodent.
The raspy cry of a jack rabbit.
Madness, or a hair's
breadth from it, Fantasy
in C Major. There are
no wolves here. The man
across the way stuffed one
for target practice. Up close,
you can see the holes, *the wholly*
enlightened earth radiant
with triumphant calamity.
My neighbor watches from inside.
Carnivore incarnate,
wolves. Five falling
stepwise notes. Choirs
of angels, demons. Shade
and nuance. A long, drawn,
wavering howl.

Ars Poetica

TAXIDERMIST in block-letters
on a plywood sign beside the highway.
We're just an hour now from home. My son's
head bobs to the beat behind his headphones. A fox—
ears pricked, nose frozen mid-quiver, one paw lifted, a thin
film of dust sometimes dulling the glass eyes—decorates
a friend's den. Road kill, he'll tell you. Only the English
let the dogs finish them off. I've watched
the hunt go out late November—horses
polished, riders' red jackets defying the fade
of autumn, hounds' tails stiff
and steady as metronomes, beating air. Their asynchronous
howls called "making music." My son
was born in a blaze of Indian summer. This morning,
he sought answers from the agency. Sealed
records released just slivers of his birth-
mother. But he fashioned a woman
from the fragments, creating her image
with such joy it swept me past
a sharp twinge of hurt into remembering
that sweet gut-rush of believing
there's someone out there
who completely understands you. And so, I couldn't
begrudge this tongue and groove fit imagined
from scattered notes on what they share: a love
of sports and music, green eyes, eczema. Flies.
I'm sure there were flies my friend
waved away to check the damage. We almost never,
he told me once, see a fox. It's the gallop

we love. That must have been what gave him—
squatting in shirtsleeves over the carcass,
heat and stench rising from the asphalt—
the stomach to scrape it up.

The Star

Its white blaze startles
from the forehead of the new
brown calf who, curious,
turns from his mother to look
as I ramble past. Marked
or anointed? Is there
a difference? Even without
the bull's-eye, the calf is meant
for slaughter. He turns back
to nurse, indifferent, as I head
home to my own children.
On the sidewalks at school,
this April, they've written poems
in chalk—pink, blue, yellow—
Li Po, Dickinson, Pound.
Every day, the words wearing away
a little more beneath our feet
until we're walking
on Sappho's fragments, all
we know of her. The deep,
unseemly gaps, a slate
scattered with spent blossoms,
the students busy moving on
to something else.

The Shetland

Interrupted mid-call, the librarian drops the phone
when his assistant pops the office door to ask:

Would the library like a pony? A lady at the front desk
       has brought one in.

A paint.
It grazes in the stacks, looks content to wait for his decision.

The adult bending to the child. Russian kale
purpling in the pot out back,

useless and beautiful. You think I'm making this up, but I'm not.
Although, the pony, life-size, is stuffed,
                      the librarian's pulse quickens

for the few seconds he thinks it flesh and blood. Until now,

his day has not been good. So many

books to care for, story times to schedule, readers to inspire,
and always the muse, balking halter, lead and whip, comes
only when she chooses.

There is a problem

with the goat appliqué on her pink-striped shirt,
the little girl points out. The horns—
antlers with branches here and there—
puzzling to a child who believes
these are goats instead of reindeer,
imagines the bleat and frolic
of billies, kids, nannies. A Heidi
in the city saving the soft rolls
for grandmother. When I first read
that tale, I had no knowledge
of hard bread. You could curl
the Wonder I ate into a tiny ball.
But this girl's in a bank, waiting.
Her folks trying to save their home.
Yes, I say to her, I see,
as she puffs out her chest.
Goat's milk is much kinder
to your stomach. Heidi drank it
by the bucketful. I could tell her
how red fades to pink
with each washing, and no matter
what you call it, each thing
remains what it is.

One of the Slow Cats

I offer a hand quickly met by a wave
of nose, spine, tail. Some Siamese in the pointy face.
"Bojangles" on a frayed blue collar.
One of the slow cats. Barely visible
through a tangle of jasmine and live oak,
the weathered brown of a frame house.
I've never seen the owner, just the handmade
"Slow Cat Crossing" sign. You would laugh,
if you were here, the different ways it could be
read. That last summer, freckled, legs
propped on the deck railing, scotch
in hand, you babbled on about your mother,
shopping, the weather, children. Cancer
was in all four quadrants, the doctors said later,
epithelial ovarian tumors growing, dividing,
wandering. A car is coming.
The cat trots off across the road,
so goddamn cocksure.

Eve: After the Fall

The stone has fallen from the bee box,
the hive is loosed,
                the music started,

& a child wearing glitter
in her hair, a sprinkle of barrettes,
sequins on her slippers,
whirls in bright hands-over-head abandon.

The gods had covered their ears to me
& cried, *Enough.*

So much drudgery & drivel to suffer through alone.

But then one day my dryer lint
                was the palest lavender.

I molded it with glue into a tiny man.

Hands shaping hands, flesh sculpting flesh,
we were somewhere between
                beautiful & ugly
when he first drew breath.

Three AM

Awake on the flip side,
streetlights block the stars.

The moon's lost
behind somebody's roof.

Marking time: the ice maker,
a car on the street,

the whoosh of furnace
on then off. A monk

bending over a flower,
sees crucifixion, sacrifice,

names it passion. Passiflora.
Christ. A woman

should have the right
to choose her own fetters,

black nylons and a whip.
Wet them, she says

on late-night TV, the ropes.
They'll shrink as they dry,

bind even tighter. And here,
a gag—but he's gone,

her young lover,
disappeared off screen,

her door left standing ajar.
Monster, his parting shot.

It's a sign of winter,
the setting of the Pleiades,

passion flower extract
in a glass. A gentle remedy,

the bottle says, to help
with sleep. I swallow

drop after bitter drop.
Not a hair stirs, the beast

already nodding off.

At the Boundary of Desire

Count to ten,
   Once I saw a woman spray-painted white.
roll the ball with each beat.
   White panties, two white fig leaves—
Miss a step
   and it's back to the beginning.
One, two . . .
   ceramic—over her breasts.
Good job, I tell her.
   Closing her eyes,
Good job, she says again and again.
   she posed as a statue in the piazza.
Sometimes,
   she even looks at me.
But if I reach to touch her . . .
   Crowds passed by.
she's gone, lost
   They dropped money
in an autistic spin,
   in her cardboard box.
arms planed, eyes turned inward.
   She centrifuges me out of her world.
If you touched her
   marble finish,
the surface would give like overripe fruit,
   paint would flake.
So I never touch her,
   No one ever touched her,
sweet apple dangling still.

Open Water

They push on through the swells,
the swimmers off La Jolla.
We track them by the colors of their caps
to the buoy and back, caught up
in the race. Today
you clasped my wrist gently
and told me you were sorry.
It's a small thing, what you have done,
a petty grievance. The swimmers
shake off the wet as they emerge,
the winners lining up.
Harbor seals have claimed
the beach at Children's Pool,
fouled the sand. Some view it
as a crime, but still the tourists come.
How fast, yesterday,
we journeyed out to see the whales,
our small boat bucking chop
as we searched through the binoculars
for spray. I can't forgive you
yet—there's too much pleasure
hanging in the balance.
The sun licks moisture
from the breeze and salts our skin.
A dolphin leaps—as if we could forget
what teems below the surface.

Battle City

Dark Magician Girl, her strength
increases. Multiply the points, 500 times

the number of cards
in all players' graveyards. I think

it's a bad idea—the number 13
painted large and black

on the yellow-green ambulance
I'm following. Al's heart—

as we stop and go in traffic,
no flashing lights or siren—

must still beat. *Stay Back
500 Feet.* Dark Magician Girl—

the first to tell Yugi and Yami
what they're up against. The single

snake in blue on the left rear door.
At least they got that right,

the staff of Asclepius, medicine
and healing—dear god

we pray for Al—not the caduceus,
Mercury's magic wand.

Messenger, conductor of the dead,
the god of theft holds two serpents

fucking on a wingèd stick.
What's your name? the medics asked.

Aspirin. Oxygen. Blood pressure.
Breathe. *Who's President?*

What day is it? Dark Magician Girl,
Ka of Mana, apprentice

of Mahado, Shadow Games
threaten to destroy us all.

Where is the brave
and powerful Pharaoh?

Help him battle his way out
of the virtual world. *Emergency*

Entrance. Al unloaded
on the dock, whisked away

through automated doors,
while I'm called in to fill out forms.

Fort Worden

Olympic Peninsula, Washington

Cliffside, above currents the locals portage
to avoid, each weekend couples exchange vows.
No matter that the Scottish tower
no bride ever graced rises like a middle finger
on the path there and back.
A housewife secured with a bow
was once in every soldier's duffel—
the standard issue mending kit.
Squint, thread the eye, repair.
Sew one ragged edge to the other. Forget
combat. The men buried here
died of Spanish influenza, and the fort,
now packed with Winnebagos,
never fired a hostile shot. Each morning,
from the battery that holds the high bluff,
I lob a captured sunrise cross continent
to your phone—work keeping you
back East. Beyond this point,
the Salish Sea gentles into waterways
so intricate and intertwined, they need
to be protected. Debris washing up
on shore, invasive species.
Our vows a keepsake on cassette
tucked somewhere in a drawer.

Revelations

Behold, I send you forth as sheep in the midst of wolves.

—*Matthew 10:16*

i.   The Care and Keeping of Scorpions

No matter how venomous, if a scorpion
breathes Sicily's air,

it will die immediately. I imagine
holding one on a flattened palm,

approaching the island on a boat.
How close before it starts

convulsing? The doorbell rings.
A man on the stoop, a woman

three steps behind. *My wife,* he says,
with a bow in her direction.

And did I know the Bible predicted
all the Horrors of the Modern World?

He clutches a worn copy to his chest.
His wife nods, face pale.

I'm sorry, I say, and shut the door.
Do you believe that shit? The Internet

says Sicily is full of scorpions.
Euscorpius sicanus under stones,

in the cracks and crevices of old
casas, villas. This book is dated 1963.

The waning days of Dick and Jane,
Spot and Puff, pass me an ashtray,

dear. Scorpius survives, crawls across
the southern sky, picks up airborne

vibrations, locates prey, feeds
on its own kind. Blessed—*be not*

afraid—are the clinically detached.

ii.   He Said: Walk with Me

I work in space. A great pickup line
if there ever was one. My girlfriend

checks out copyrights, credits for TV
biographies. Her makeup is flawless,

menthol jelly on her lips and eyelids.
We smear into each other.

Send Lazarus that he may dip the tip
of his finger in water and cool my tongue.

Tremendous heat resideth
in heavenly bodies. Stars form,

evolve, explode. I pick over
the wreckage, cool down Mars

with the doves of Venus. Praise
empties from church windows.

A woman idles by the curb, gathering
amens, blessed be's, faith, hope,

and love like pennies pitched
in the dust. On her lap, the black

Gideon stolen from a hotel drawer.
You're standing at the edge

of your skin, I know, but I will do
nothing for that woman

but chronicle her obsessive
behavior. Leave her there, gambling

on God. God knows her mother
tried. Think of her as an amuse-bouche.

The air thins on the rise up.
There are limits to what I can carry.

iii.   The Gospel Chicken House

God's light shines on the chicken house,
the sunflowers out back, sacks

pulled over their heads, twist–tied
to keep the birds from feeding.

Fifteen hundred nights and counting,
God's right here in the chicken house with us.

Animals drop when they drop.
The woman belts out her song,

goes *where roses never fade,* and all God's
people say amen. The spangles

on her jacket like diamonds.
The deer hits the fence running,

busts the top board with its chest.
Welcome to Saturday night live

at the chicken house. Have a hot dog.
Sarah makes the pies. *God holds*

the thread of life. Can't you feel the tug?
Forty by one hundred, we can seat

three fifty. Listen for the "alter" call.
Canada geese just passing through,

a swarm of suicidal moths.
God watch all the dead children

in thy tender care. Turn off
that inner monologue and sing.

These are cramped quarters.
God lit the torch and handed it to us.

Holding for the Farrier

On fire, he might think he's on fire,
Thomas says, right before touching
the power of Anthanor and a blaze red shoe
to the horse's foot. Widening
my stance, I grip the halter tight, brace
for a startled bolt. But there's only a brief
soft-lipped nudge to my hand.
Steam engulfs us.
                    Balneum vaporis,
fire and dragons. Again the anvil
sings. Alchemy, its tinctures, mixtures,
inunctions bought a carriage, four teams
of horses for Leonhard Thurneysser
zum Thurm of Bile. Oleum cinnamoni
he sold for 12 thalers, and amethyst, sapphire
remedies yielded fantastic returns. Work
as a physician only earned him feed.
Thomas pounds iron, sparks
showers of constellations, realizes
Cauda Pavonis, and muttering:
You can't make money at this,
under his breath
sends us again
                into vapors. Mercury conceives
inward Sulpher, coagulates itself. The sun
and moon merge, have a child, Hermaphrodite.
Eyebrows delicate, butterfly arched. Nails
long, slick and lavender. A curvaceous, comatose
beautician pulled from the wreckage yielded

strange fruit.
                         Similia similibus curantur. And EMTs,
surprised by the cock and balls under the dress,
backed away. *Mocked him*
today's newspaper claimed. Thurneysser fled
when gold leaf chipped off the lead he'd sold
as pure gold. The beautician died. Mocked *her,*
the protesters corrected. Always
use the pronoun describing the gender
presentation.
                    Thomas separates the quintessence,
likes his women perfumed and coiffed. This horse,
he says, had an abscess. Props
the foot on his leather apron, points
out the rupture high on the hoof wall. I rub
my finger over the hard protrusion. Sharp
shoots of pain imagined
up my own leg.
                   Manifestation of the negative
aspect. The horse nuzzles my shoulder, my hand
patting an apology for not knowing. Language.
Thurneysser wrote in languages
he didn't know. The Devil
in his inkpot. Divorce cost him all
his money. Cold mornings, Thomas's first wife
started his truck, warmed the cab to comfort.
Lying in bed, once, he heard
a girlfriend coaxing a reluctant roar
out of his Chevy.
                  Stygian darkness.
It's over, he says, *when girlfriends act
like wives.* One last blast,
unctuous water, hot mist. *Tough*

old guy, Thomas offers, *took care of it*
himself. Cheiron convulsing in pain, fever
dripping sweat from flesh to fur, hooves
trying to pace away the agony inflicted
by a friend, traded immortality to end
his suffering. Catholicism. Thurneysser
converted when silver wouldn't transmute
to gold. *He'll be sore,* Thomas says,
for a few days. The horse steps gingerly,
bends to nibble fresh hay in his stall. Thomas loads
the truck, clangs the anvil onto the steel bed.
Heavy and dark, it waits there.

Mrs. Cannon Passes the Parthenon
on Her Way Home from Work

The tree limbs are black and bare. They spider the concrete
   aggregate
of Nashville's Parthenon. Mrs. Cannon's limo floats
down West End. A black bear
                          somewhere,
concrete, one paw raised as if hailing a cab, is one of the city's
   seven
wonders. She forgets the others.
January.
         The creek in her front yard
is cold, rocky, gargles on
past the governor's mansion next door. When spring comes, its
   water
will run clear, clean fingers through waves of sweetgrass. Ophelia.
She is Sarah Ophelia Cannon. The battered
straw bonnet, dangling $1.98 price tag, cheap ruffled dress and
   scuffed Mary Janes,
left behind at the studio. Her breast prostheses
                            itch, shift. The
                            horizontals,
none of them
at the Parthenon are straight.
A slight curve in the middle gives the illusion of perfection. And the
   verticals,
the Doric columns, bulge widest a third of the way up.
                            Cancer.
                            Hee Haw
                            and how-
                            dee.

Grinder's Switch didn't have cancer. No Watergate nor Vietnam
  neither.

But Minnie Pearl has cancer. Hard
and unforgiving as any Opry bench.
Fingering her brooch, Mrs. Cannon ponders
                                    the science of
                                    fundraising.
They're gilding Athena. Gold, forty feet of her, will tower just
  inside
the heaviest bronze doors in the world. The Parthenon experience
will be complete. Minnie's still looking
for a "feller." Mrs. Cannon's husband likes cigars.
                                            Charity.
The Cancer Ball. Old money can dig deep. She wants to
lie down when she gets home,
                          dream about the best jokes she
                          ever told.
Waiting, full-length and formal, her blue silk, the matching satin
  shoes.

With a Delicate Flicker of the Fan

Milky galaxies pulled apart: the broken
stars, patchy ground glass & dark mysteries

of my asymptomatic lungs
unveiled on screen. I held, going

through the donut hole, my breath, the rapid
whip around of tiny cameras, whir,

whiz, snapping every angle to reveal
Lady Windermere's Disease. How lovely—

flutter, blush—a name I could drop over
tea & crumpets graciously, that would not

stop traffic. The raw inflammatory
processes from fastidious,

habitual, suppression of the cough.
Such painless penetration: Take a deep breath,

hold, breathe, surrender to test after test,
the savages of age. We are fading, husband,

you & I. Legs intertwined,
sheets starched, the rigid tug of

hospital corners, bronchiec [stasis]—
can you sense how my body, man-of-pause,

has turned against me, my mother hiding
behind the curtains? Why does medicine

have to be so dry? A moment ago,
my arms wet with roses for the blue bowl,

we were talking about children, carpets
on the terrace, compromise, the white hand–

kerchief falling. *Hush,*
you say, shutting the fan's lace, mesh,

wooden ribs, *hush,*
as slowly your hands unfasten

me—the harsh afternoon light, layer upon layer
of pit & precipice falling away,

until we both surface catching our breath
as if we had been swimming

a long, long time underwater.

Snapped

Her daughters shocked
to a splay-footed
standstill,
hair bows askew,
ears cocked as if wary
of what's happening
behind them. 1914
and the family fruitcake
recipe says:
blanche the almonds,
shell pecans,
crystallize the cherries,
then call a man
to stir the heavy batter.
But they are too full
of four- and six-year-old
giggles and squirms
to pose pretty and smile
for their mama
who has finally snapped,
Turn around
and face the bushes!
and is taking a picture
of the backs
of their new white
summer Sunday dresses,
of the rows of tiny bone
buttons scavenged
from an old blouse,
the flounces crocheted

by kerosene light,
the cropped sleeves
trimmed with lace bartered
from the pack-peddler
for a skillet supper
and a spare bed. No
running water, electricity,
phones or paved roads; no
self-timer to unchain her
from the tripod; no
click and share,
but one snapshot
and generations of us
see: This is a woman
who could wield a needle.

Flight

Bird, I think, waking to a dark flutter
then no—adrenaline rush—
bat. Vampire, rabies. *Don't kill it,*
the wildlife HELP guy begs me on the phone.
Gentle, he says. *Intelligent. Consumes
mosquitos.* Later, the colony,
fifty plus adults, pups, found nestled
in the attic's louvered vent, a rip
in the screen. Bats always return
to the same roost. *Shhhhhhh,*
Mother would say. *The children.
What they don't know . . .* A painting over
the bullet-sized patch in the plaster,
carpet covering the blood-stained floor—
I've been haunted unawares before. Capture
the intruder with a shoe box, slide
cardboard underneath, hold at arms-length,
carry outside, release. A wonder, their wings,
five-fingered hands adapted for flight.
Big Brown, Little Brown, Evening? HELP guy
wants to know. Two of the three species
at risk. I don't look close enough
to tell. Imagine the dart and dive at dusk,
wing, claw, fang tangled in my hair. *A myth,*
he sighs. Explains: *forage, food,
echolocation.* But even after I learned
the truth, I never asked her name—
grandfather's first wife who shot herself upstairs—

or why. Set up a one-way exit,
repair the screen—
welded wire mesh, heavy duty stainless steel.

Giant Echiums

West Cork, Ireland

Not native, they tower ten to twenty feet,
have invasive habits,

blue flowers—
bees pleasure them in swarms,

the inflorescence bubbling like
champagne. Cheers. *Slainte.* How easy

to fit in. Not far from here
the Famine burial pit, nine thousand

casketless remains. Some lost
ancestral ties, perhaps. Another

interloper, fuchsia, rampant
in this mild, moist climate

from the North Atlantic drift,
crowds the lane. Today,

the headlines are diaspora, Syrian,
thousands flooding into Europe.

The glebe a garden now
that charges for admission.

The field a somersault of bulbs—
someone planted onions

upside down. Roots
twist toward gravity, foliage seeks

the sun. Mostly, I keep my hands
in the dirt, pull up stinging nettles

until my fingers numb.

Visiting the Thorne Miniatures

Apple blossoms?
I squint at a spray of white
flowers on a table against the far wall.

Daylight's illusion puddles the floor
of the English entrance hall. The tiny front door
stands open. A pair of riding gloves on the windowsill.

I want to go to your *house,* the boy says
tugging the ponytailed man who peers through the window
next to mine—the French boudoir.

Look, the man says,
is your room at home as big as this?
The boy flattens his nose against the glass.

My whole house isn't as big as that,
the boy laughs, swinging from the rail.
His tight coffee curls brush my sleeve.

I slide over to the Charleston ballroom.
The settee's legs a fine-grained
mahogany carved with a jeweler's lathe.

We've been here all day. The boy bounces
in the aisle. *I want to go
to* your *house.*

A chandelier quivers with crystals
the size of pinheads. Small is charming,

it invites you to play god.

A grandfather clock by the stairs
houses a dot-sized pendulum
I will to swing.

The man balls his hands in his pockets.
This outing . . . I think each had imagined it
differently—the boy, the man.

Down for the Count

Letting mono run its course, asleep for weeks
in the infirmary, I missed the lecture
on Apollinaire, walk alone to the bridge
years later, inhaling coffee, diesel
fumes. He tried to catch me up, Professor P.,
a wreck in love himself. The wife who left
him willow tall, a wraith—nagging, bitter.
Parsing poems that day, autumn's dark
against the window, his face a shadow—
I still don't understand the man, the kissing
disease that laid me low, how much was
constancy, how much defiance. Boring, flat
and green, Mirabeau Bridge looks functional
and sturdy, and Paris is so wicked cold.

Freeze

Chicago

Not mine, those teenage boys playing chicken on the tracks.
And it's been decades since I lived two train stops south
or Lake Michigan has frozen all the way across. The 2:04
just coming into view. *Stop,* I want to say to them,
but don't. Late winter, and the water's startled blue
is as lovely as it is concerning. I've no illusions
of control. At night, those snowpack years, as I trudged back
to my apartment, the lamp-lit homes would offer up
their dreams, and I could see through each cracked curtain
what I wanted to believe. Now, the moon's too often tangled
in the trees, and the lake has given up its seasons. The train
has come and gone. The boys have tired of their game,
and I can go on about my errands. No one admitted fear,
no child was lost, our luck held firm. But touch me
and I will break into unspoken prayers, littering this icy walk.

April & the Affront of Spring

Last month, Ellen, shot
at twenty-two. A random
campus act (police assure),
that makes the evening
news. Her dad, until
that moment, just a guy
I knew at school
who stole flowers
from the park to woo
my roommate. Pink, clipped
branches from the cherries
that grew so close
together each tree's
blossoms blended
with the next. And today,
Allen. The cause,
my son at college
e-mails home,
an accidental overdose.
The chancellor's note
that follows—full of measures
they will take to ease
the students' grief.
It's not contagious,
my son said earnestly
at eight, leaning toward me
from his chair, too small
yet for his feet to reach
the ground. His classmate
Alex crumpling

to the floor that day
heart-stopped during
jumping jacks, a fatal defect
lurking hidden. But not
contagious, his teachers
reassured. This disaster
could not spread
from one child to the next.

Girls, She Falcons, Be Thin: Let Us
Work Ourselves Asleep Against You

—A.R. Ammons, *Sphere*

"Don't do it," the falconer says,
when I confess
the overwhelming urge
to pet the bird, stroke
its feathers. A virgin,
my mother told me
as a child, is someone
no one's ever touched.
And so the raptor,
who never felt her mother's
tender preening,
views contact
as attack,
responds with beak
and talon to even the gentlest
caress. Strange angel
of the mews, almost weightless
on the glove,
she will snap
the songbird's back
to satisfy her hunger, wrench
flesh from bone. Her fierce
appetite harnessed
to feed our own, her sharp-eyed
intent—so different
from the soft stirrings
I felt as a girl, innocent
and ignorant. The limp yellow

carcass of a chick
tossed skyward, the peregrine
quick on the draw, the bait
caught mid-fall in a storm
of down. She mantles
meat as a mother
might shelter a child, merciless
in its protection. I was
never a virgin
by my mother's definition,
and as a youth thought
chastity a curse. The falcon tethered
to her perch,
cloistered in her dark
and isolated room. But now,
I've come to marvel
at her stoops, her high-speed
strikes, the fury unleashed
in her pursuit
of prey. Hail Mary
full of grace, Artemis and Isis,
wings folded, blinded quiet,
she tilts an ear
to the field's
great reservoir of sky,
then hood removed,
the jesses loosed,
she slips the fist to rise.

Notes

"Ruins, Trophies, Palms":
    The title is the original name of the three movements in Schumann's
    Fantasy in C Major.

    The third phrase in italics is adapted from the following quote from
    Theodor Adorno and Max Horkheimer's book, *Dialectic of Enlightenment:*
    "Enlightenment, understood in the widest sense as the advance of
    thought, has always aimed at liberating human beings from fear and
    installing them as masters. Yet the wholly enlightened earth is radiant
    with triumphant calamity."

"Battle City":
    Dark Magician Girl, Yugi, Yami and the Pharaoh are characters in the
    Yu-Gi-Oh Japanese anime series.

"Mrs. Cannon Passes the Parthenon on Her Way Home from Work":
    Sarah Ophelia Cannon developed the comedic character Minnie Pearl,
    a spinster from the mythical small town of Grinder's Switch who was
    obsessed with chasing men and gossip. Mrs. Cannon made her debut at
    the Grand Ole Opry in 1940 and continued performing until her death
    in 1991.

    Regarding the Parthenon: Nashville, Tennessee calls itself "The Athens
    of the South," and a full-sized replica of the Parthenon, including a
    statue of Athena, is located in the city's Centennial Park.

"Visiting the Thorne Miniatures":
    Mrs. James Ward Thorne's collection of 68 miniature rooms is a
    permanent exhibit at the Art Institute of Chicago.

Acknowledgments

Grateful acknowledgment is made to the editors of the following journals where some of these poems, or versions of them, first appeared:

420pus: "Starlings"

The 2River View: "No Rain for a Spell," "Open Water"

Able Muse: "Down for the Count"

Alaska Quarterly Review: "Fort Worden"

Barrow Street: "There is a problem"

Bellevue Literary Review: "Sunday"

Beloit Poetry Journal: "Snapped"

Blackbird: "Holding for the Farrier," "Mrs. Cannon Passes the Parthenon on Her Way Home from Work," and "Three AM"

The Carolina Quarterly: "For My Son's Birth Mother" (as "A Tender Dance")

Diode: "At the Boundary of Desire," "One of the Slow Cats," and "With a Delicate Flicker of the Fan" (as "In the Victorian Language of the Fan")

The Hudson Review: "The Star" (as "Ice Melts, Wings Grow")

The Louisville Review: "Ars Poetica"

The Massachusetts Review: "Girls, She Falcons, Be Thin: Let Us Work Ourselves Asleep Against You"

New Orleans Review: "Wake"

Oxford American: "April & the Affront of Spring"

Poetry East: "The Shetland"

The Southern Review: "Eve: After the Fall," and "Undone"

storySouth: "Revelations"

Streetlight Magazine: "How to Grow Wild"

Whiskey Island Magazine: "Weeding"

Willow Springs: "Freeze"

The following poems or some version of them appeared in the chapbook *Holding for the Farrier,* published by Finishing Line Press: "Late Summer," "Visiting the Thorne Miniatures," "Sunday," "Three AM," "Revelations," "Holding for the Farrier," "Mrs. Cannon Passes the Parthenon on Her Way Home from Work," "Battle City," "Ruins, Trophies, Palms" (as "Beginning in D Minor") and "Ars Poetica."

Many thanks to my teachers David Wojahn, Gregory Donovan, Elizabeth Seydel Morgan and Roselyn Elliott and to fellow writers Maria Hagan, Craig Beaven, Patty Paine, Susan Williams, Tara Bray, Allen Chamberlain, Elizabeth Cooper, Lynda Fleet Perry, Stuart Gravatt, Kirsten Gray, Catherine MacDonald, Leslie Shiel, Lorraine Waltz and the late Susan Early for supporting my work through the years. I am very grateful to the Virginia Center for the Creative Arts (with special thanks to Carole Weinstein for a residency fellowship), the Ragdale Foundation, Centrum and Porches for the quiet space to write many of these poems, to Lesley Wheeler for selecting Passiflora and to Caron Andregg and all at Cider Press Review. And most of all, thank you to Bob, Bryson and Mick, whose love and encouragement made everything possible.